14 GENESEE STREET
CAMILLUS, NEW YORK 13031

Bridgestone
B O O K S

Life in the World's Biomes

Polar Plants

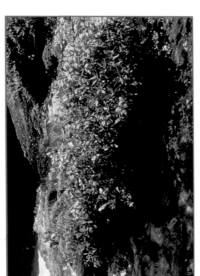

by Catherine A. Welch

Consultant:
Ian A. Ramjohn, PhD
Department of Botany and Microbiology
University of Oklahoma
Norman, Oklahoma

CAMILLUS

Capstone
press

Mankato, Minnesota

Bridgestone Books are published by Capstone Press,
151 Good Counsel Drive, P.O. Box 669, Mankato, Minnesota 56002.
www.capstonepress.com

Library of Congress Cataloging-in-Publication Data
Welch, Catherine A.
Polar plants / by Catherine A. Welch.
p. cm.—(Bridgestone Books. Life in the world's biomes)
Summary: "Tells about a variety of polar plants, how they are used, why they are in danger, and
how they are being protected"—Provided by publisher.
Includes bibliographical references and index.
ISBN 0-7368-4320-5 (hardcover)
1. Plants—Polar regions—Juvenile literature. I. Title. II. Series: Life in the world's biomes.
QK473.5.W45 2006
581.7'586—dc22
2004029139

Editorial Credits

Amber Bannerman, editor; Jennifer Bergstrom, designer; Kelly Garvin, photo researcher;
Scott Thoms, photo editor

Photo Credits

Ann & Rob Simpson, cover (flower in foreground)
Bruce Coleman Inc./Dotte Larsen, 20; Fritz Polking, 6 (left); Mark Newman, 16; Tui De Roy, 4,
6 (bottom right), 10
Corbis/Philip Gould, 14; Tom Bean, 18
Corel, 1
Getty Images Inc./Alan Kearney, cover (background)
Gilbert S. Grant, 12
Minden Pictures/Michio Hoshino, 6 (top right)
Nature Picture Library/Asgeir Helgestad, 8

The author thanks Judith Stark, Jacqueline Hoffman, Joan Stokes, and the staff of the Southbury,
Connecticut, library for their assistance in gathering material for this book.

1 2 3 4 5 6 10 09 08 07 06 05

Table of Contents

Polar Regions

Near the North and South poles lie the coldest regions on earth. The Arctic **tundra** is near the North Pole. Antarctica surrounds the South Pole. Both the Arctic and Antarctica are cold, dry deserts. Most years, polar snowfall is less than 60 inches (152 centimeters). That amount is equal to 6 inches (15 centimeters) of rain.

Polar areas have long, dark winters. Most plants cannot grow during winter's bitterly cold and dry weather. These plants grow during the shorter, warmer summer months.

▼ Snowstorms sometimes hit polar areas during the summer and cover plants.

Polar Plants

In summer, plants brighten the Arctic. The top layer of soil thaws. The Arctic land becomes wet and squishy. Willow shrubs grow along rivers. Fluffy, white flowers grow on top of cotton grass. Yellow Arctic poppies and purple saxifrage add color to the land.

In Antarctica, plants grow along warmer coasts. **Moss** forms on packed mud, sand, and fine gravel. Flowering hair grass and pearlwort grow in small clumps.

◀ Cotton grass (left), yellow Arctic poppies and moss campion (top right), and moss (bottom right) grow in polar regions.

Polar Plant Features

Polar plants have ways to stay alive during strong winds. Icy polar winds can rip plants to shreds. Some polar plants grow in large groups. The outside plants **protect** the middle plants from the wind. Short plants hold tight to the ground, so they don't get blown away.

Polar plants also have ways of staying alive during the cold winters. Some plants live only as seeds during this time. They bloom in the summer. In most polar plants, **sap** does not freeze. If it froze, plant stems would burst.

▼ The white saxifrage plant's low height protects it from polar wind.

Plant Homes for Animals

Antarctic animals use polar plants for their nests. Albatross birds make nests out of grass and mud. Sheathbills are birds that use grass and moss to build their nests.

Arctic animals use polar plants for warmth and shelter. Ground squirrels line their winter sleeping holes with dry grass. Arctic lemmings use grass and feathers for their underground nests.

▼ An albatross sits on its nest in Antarctica.

Plant Foods for Animals

Polar plants are food for some Arctic animals. Arctic squirrels dig up grasses and flowers with their sharp claws. Berries are food for grizzly bears and foxes.

Antarctic plants are food for some insects and birds. Springtails are tiny insects that live on land. These insects live inside tightly packed clumps of mosses and **lichens**. Springtails eat plant bits at the soil's surface. Antarctic gulls and other birds sometimes eat land plants too.

▼ Arctic ground squirrels use their sharp claws to help them eat.

Plants Used by People

People can use polar plants for fun. Club moss **spores** can be used in fireworks. People watch as these spores help fireworks explode with a flash. Some people use club moss branches to make holiday wreaths.

Some polar plants are healthy to eat. Arctic summer berries are healthy foods. Bilberries and blueberries may help blood flow to the skin and eyes. These berries are also used to make jam. Young leaves of Arctic willows are high in vitamin C.

⬇ Club moss spores are found at the tips of branches.

Polar Plants in Danger

Pollution harms polar plants. Factories, homes, and cars burn coal and oil that give off harmful gases. These gases rise into the air. The wind carries the gases to polar regions. The gases can kill polar plants.

Some polar plant areas are in danger. Global climate changes have made polar regions warmer. The warmer weather has caused more shrubs to grow. Shrubs block rain and light from small plants such as lichens. Lichens have no roots and need rainwater to live.

▼ Pulp mills, and other factories, can give off gases that pollute the air.

19

Protecting Polar Plants

People everywhere can protect polar plants. People can drive cars that give off fewer harmful gases. People can support laws to lessen pollution.

Some polar areas are protected in national parks. People are not supposed to harm or take plants from these areas. People need to keep telling lawmakers to protect polar areas. By protecting these areas, people can help polar plants continue to grow.

▼ A couple hikes in the Gates of the Arctic National Park in Alaska.

Amazing Lichens

Slow-growing lichens are amazing polar plants. They can live for thousands of years. Some lichens form crusts on rocks. Others are leafy growths.

Lichens have many uses. Branch lichens look like tiny trees. Branch lichens are used in model train sets. Reindeer lichens are the main winter food for caribou and reindeer. Scientists use lichens in air pollution studies. Lichens soak up water and chemicals from the air. If lichen growth is healthy, air quality is good.

◆ Because lichens have no roots, most attach to rocks and trees by strands called rhizines.

Glossary

lichen (LYE-ken)—a crustlike or leafy plant found on rocks and trees

moss (MAWSS)—a soft, short plant; moss covers damp soil, rocks, and tree trunks.

pollution (puh-LOO-shuhn)—harmful materials that damage the air, water, and soil

protect (pruh-TEKT)—to guard or to keep something safe from harm or injury

sap (SAP)—a watery fluid found inside plants and trees

spore (SPOR)—a small plant part that grows into a new plant; spores are produced by plants that do not flower, such as mosses and ferns.

tundra (TUHN-druh)—frozen Arctic land; mosses, lichens, and shrubs are common in tundras.

Read More

Brooks, Sheldon. *Life in the Arctic.* Life in Extreme Environments. New York: Rosen, 2004.

Pelusey, Michael, and Jane Pelusey. *Antarctica.* Continents. Philadelphia: Chelsea House Publishers, 2005.

Internet Sites

FactHound offers a safe, fun way to find Internet sites related to this book. All of the sites on FactHound have been researched by our staff.

Here's how:
1. Visit *www.facthound.com*
2. Type in this special code **0736843205** for age-appropriate sites. Or enter a search word related to this book for a more general search.
3. Click on the **Fetch It** button.

FactHound will fetch the best sites for you!

Index